Joe Woodley　　　　Leadership and Team Development Volume 2

LANDMARKS FOR MAXIMIZED SUCCESS:
LEADERSHIP AND TEAM DEVELOPMENT TRAINING SYSTEM
VOLUME 2
DIVERSITY IN THE WORKPLACE

LEADERSHIP & TEAM DEVELOPMENT SPEAKER
JOE WOODLEY

Landmarks for Success:

Volume 2

Diversity in the Workplace

Leadership and Team Members focus on developing the essential skills and behaviors appropriate for communication and interaction with today's diverse environments.

Joe Woodley	Leadership and Team Development Volume 2

TABLE OF CONTENTS

Section 1

Diversity in the Workplace

Participants will identify sources of diversity in the workplace and explore resolving potential conflicts.

Section 2

Diversity 1

Participants will acquire essential tools to resolve disputes amongst team members.

Section 3

Diversity 2

Participants will further develop essential skills to properly manage organizational disputes.

Section 4

Gender Communication

Equip participants with the resources to foster a safe working environment.

Section 5

Communication 101

Participants focus on effective communication between managerial staff and teams.

Joe Woodley   Leadership and Team Development Volume 2

Section 1

Diversity in the Workplace

What is diversity? Webster's Dictionary defines accountability as: the condition of having or being composed of differing elements : VARIETY; the inclusion of different types of people (such as people of different races or cultures) in a group or organization: an instance of being composed of differing elements or qualities

Diversity is the inescapable reality of the world we live in today. Virtually every community is comprised of a mosaic of cultures and ethnicities of peoples whose ancestral roots originate from around the world. Just as diverse as our communities are the organizations which conduct their corporate affairs in those cities and towns around the world. It is impossible to work with or for any large organization today and have no contact or communication with individuals who do not look like you, talk like you and share the same background as you.

An even more significant truth is the percentage of men and women actively participating in the workforce is dramatically changed from where it was thirty, forty and fifty years ago. Women comprise nearly fifty percent of the workforce and have surpassed their male counterparts nationally in achieving higher levels of education; elevating them to more positions of leadership and greater influence.

Leadership, teams and organizations that do not adequately equip themselves to address the changing socio-economic environments of today will find themselves incapable of meeting increased performance demands from the people they serve and eventually, discover they have become obsolete.

Diversity is an essential component not only in meeting performance demands; diversity is crucial to surpassing those demands.

Make no mistake about it: **Diversity is not going anywhere, and making the appropriate adjustments is not an option. It is a necessity.** The most diverse organizations are in position to be the best equipped and most capable at addressing productivity concerns and community needs.

NOTES:

1. In your own words, what is diversity?

_____
_____
_____

2. What are some of the ways which diversity is represented in the modern workforce?

_____
_____
_____

3. How can diversity positively impact team performance?

_____
_____
_____

4. How can diversity negatively impact team performance?

_____
_____
_____

5. Do you feel comfortable working with individuals from differing gender, racial, ethnic and economic groups?

_____
_____
_____

6. What are the best ways to build team cohesion and effectiveness, as a member in a diverse community?

   a. _____
   b. _____
   c. _____
   d. _____
   e. _____

JOURNAL

Date:_____

Section 2

Diversity 1

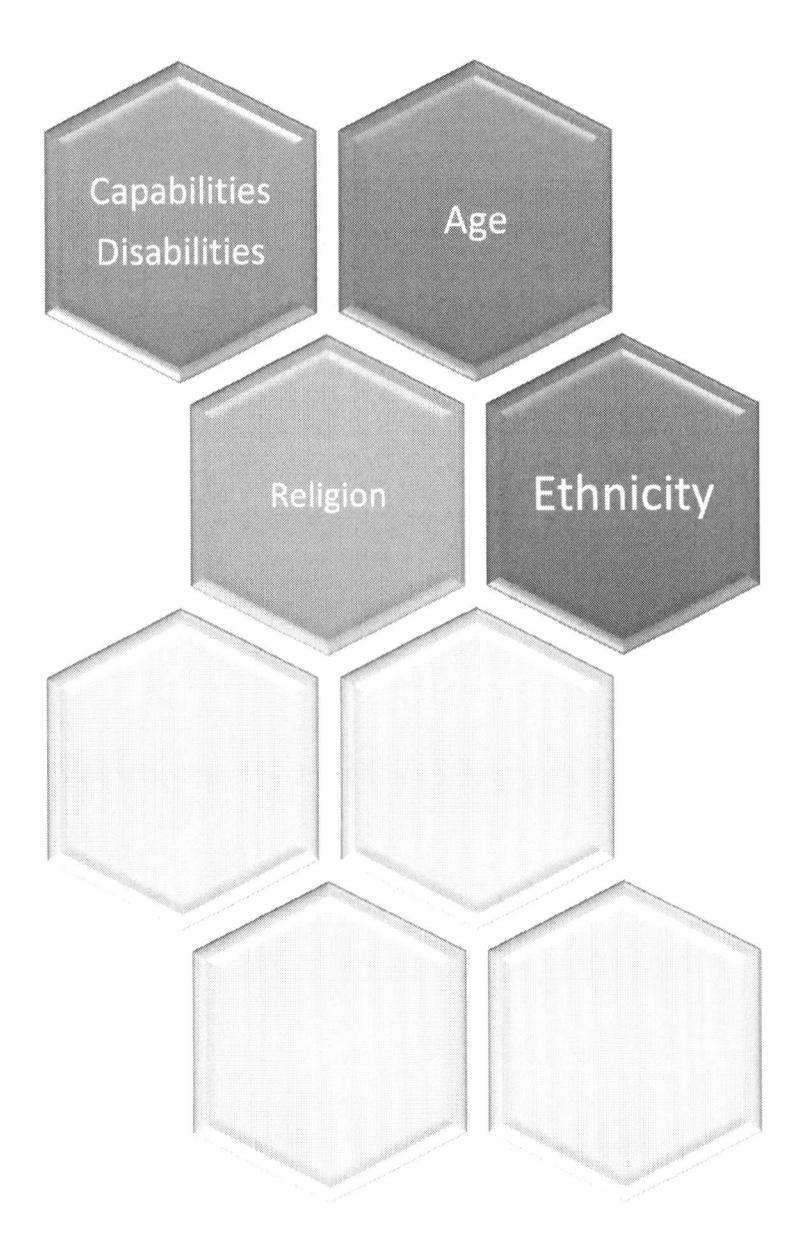

- Capabilities / Disabilities
- Age
- Religion
- Ethnicity

Types of Diversity. Diversity is about much more than race and ethnicity. Teams are comprised of individuals from various backgrounds who may have differing experiences and perspectives. These differences should not limit your ability to succeed and maximize the overall success of the team. If goals have been clearly communicated and each person understands his role is achieving those stated goals, diversity will serve to enhance the effectiveness and efficiency of the team.

When goals have not been clearly articulated, no team can perform its duties with distinction and excellence.

A diverse environment will bring its own set of challenges. Change for many people can be difficult, most especially when you have not been exposed to, or worked with persons who do not share the same point of view on a variety of topics, including work related issues. The goal of diversity training is not to get you to change your viewpoint; rather to respect and accept others who do not share your worldview. Discrimination based on anything other than poor work performance in the workplace is never acceptable and should not be tolerated.

In this section, we will discuss three types of diversity and their potential impact in the workplace.

Capabilities Disabilities: Most people have a strong desire to work and be a contributing member of society. People that live with a disability are no different. Individuals with disabilities are persons whose physical, mental, cognitive, or developmental condition impairs, interferes with, or limits their ability to engage in certain tasks or actions or participate in typical daily activities and interactions. Limited abilities do not mean lazy, incompetent or incapable.

If the person can perform the job assigned to them, they should be treated with all due respect and given every opportunity to succeed and positively impact the trajectory of the team and organization.

Age: Organizations have becoming increasingly diverse in age demographics. This is an excellent opportunity to tap into the knowledge and wisdom of persons who are more experienced and established team members. Younger team members may be better adept in the newer technological advances. The wisdom accumulated through experience and the energy provided through youth are a powerful one-two punch. Both groups need each other to meet the demands of today's high performance society.

Religion: The third rail of discussion in many settings is religion or theology. I would like to include politics in this section as well. It is irresponsible and irrational to expect that theology and politics will never come up as a point of discussion. No matter where I have served, those topics have always come up, most especially during an election year. Religious theology and political differences should never be used as a weapon to disrespect and dishonor team members and leadership. A person's inclusion or exclusion should not be determined by his chosen political party or minor theological differences.

Ethnicity: Ethnic Diversity has much more to do with cultural similarities and differences than racial similarities and differences. For example, a man and a woman of two different racial groups, who grow up next door to each other in the same economic bracket, from New York City, are likely going to have more in common than individuals raised in differing geographical communities. What one community considers a cultural norm, is not necessarily the same as another. This doesn't make the other right or wrong. It means that their experiences, have exposed them to a point of view that differs from yours.

The organization that is most successful in this century must navigate diversity effectively. Not all Asian (Oriental is Asian Art and tapestry, not individuals) people are the same. Not all Hispanics or black or white or whatever group you choose to name is the same across the board. The best way to respect people from other ethnicities is not to assume they have a particular bias. Their cultural experiences on a team are tremendously important. Relating to people from various backgrounds does not diminish organizational effectiveness. It serves the interest of the organization.

NOTES:

1. In your own words, what is the meaning of Capabilities Disabilities? Give examples of how it can benefit your organization.

_____
_____
_____

2. In your own words, what is the meaning of Age Diversity? Give examples of how it can benefit your organization.

_____
_____
_____

3. In your own words, what is Theological Diversity? Give example of how it can benefit your organization.

_____
_____
_____

4. Has there ever been a time when you witnessed someone treated differently at work because of perceived differences? How did you address the situation?

_____
_____
_____

5. Is it ever appropriate to discriminate against someone in the organization?

_____
_____
_____

6. What are some ways to address tensions in the team that may be related to "diversity"?

_____
_____
_____

JOURNAL

Date:_____

Section 3

Diversity 2

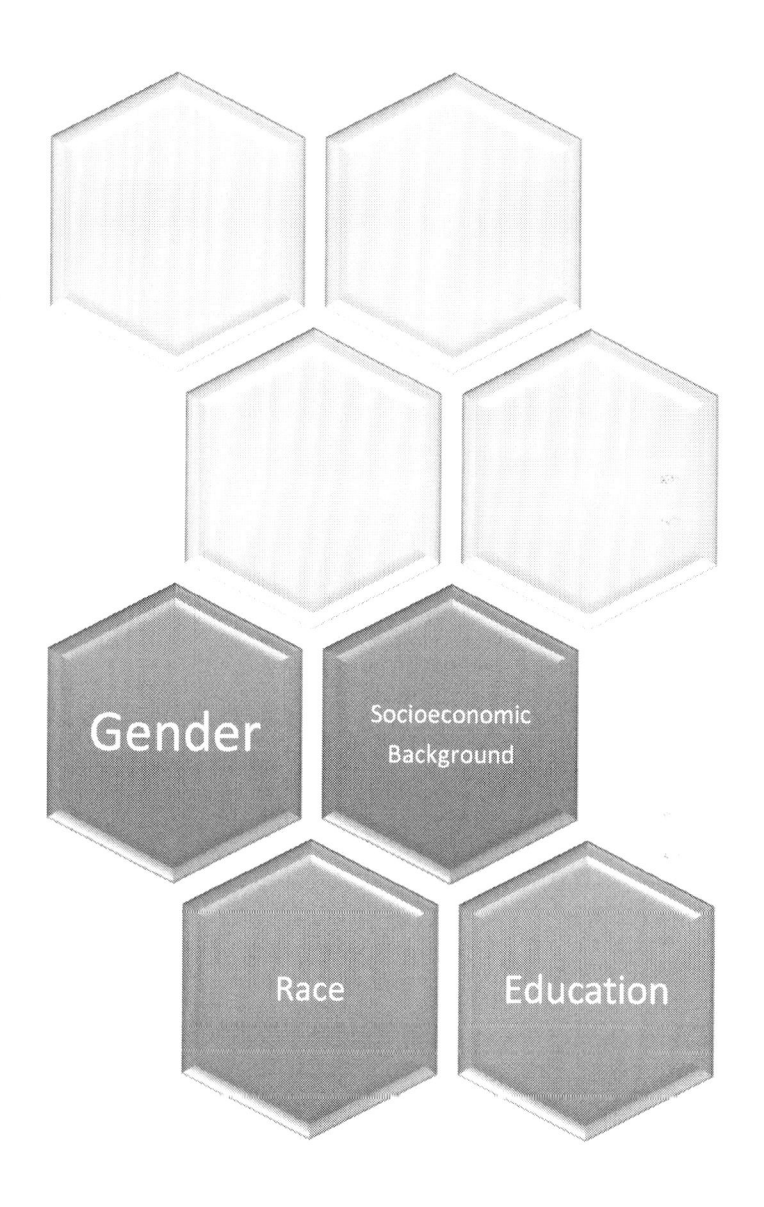

- Gender
- Socioeconomic Background
- Race
- Education

Joe Woodley   Leadership and Team Development Volume 2

Can you perform the job? The reality of the not-too-distant past is, far too often a person's ability to acquire gainful employment and achieve economic and social success was hindered by sanctioned discriminatory government policies. Although we do not live in a perfect society, there have been major strides forward in our policies and perceptions of one another as human beings. The goal should be to afford every individual the opportunities to succeed, based on his own desires and self-determination. The number one question in onboarding team members should be, is this person capable of performing or learning the prescribed functions properly?

Gender: In the year 1950, 29.6% of the workforce was female. By the year 2050, it is projected 47.7% of the workforce will be female. Gender Diversity refers to the representation of male and female participants in the workforce. More organizations are less concerned with gender as a pre-qualifier in considering the best candidates for positions. Women should be treated with the same level of respect and dignity as their male counterparts. Men and women should not be objectified by those in positions of authority, and their teammates.

Socioeconomic Background: Have you ever been discriminated against because of your economic status? Today's workforce is comprised of partnerships and teams that come from a variety of economic classes and groups. Middle class individuals team with wealthy and poorer individuals. Poorer individuals work alongside wealthier individuals. Inclusion of the best candidate for your team should not be exclusively based on the economic status. You may choose a person of a specific economic status to gain a better understanding and insight into how best to serve who you are serving, however, candidates should not be discriminated against if they are capable of fulfilling the requirements.

Race: Race is an issue that people hate to talk about. When we discuss race, we are forced to address our personal experiences, preferences and perceptions of each other; not just skin complexion. We don't like to discuss it because no one wants to say anything that can get them in trouble or publicly branded as something they are not. When we respect each other and treat one another with the same reverence we treat ourselves, then race will not be the predominant issue in any organization. Prejudice, racism and any other "ism" only becomes an issue when we prejudge each other's value to the team and the organization by skin pigmentation, or some other non-job related issue.

Educational: Perhaps now, more than at any time in history, educational diversity is more valued, and more readily accepted by industry leading organizations around the world. No two individuals will have the exact educational experiences. The options and opportunities available for persons looking to increase their skillsets, and add personal value to the benefit of organizations is virtually limitless. Trade schools, mentoring, and internship programs, as well as traditional colleges and universities provide credibility, hands-on training and real-world experiences and training to prepare participants. Educational diversity serves to increase the pool of quality, and qualified team members who can help take your organization to the next level.

Disparaging stereotypes. Prejudgments, offensive language and actions are not only disallowed by most major corporations and organizations. In the United States of America, and many industrialized nations around the world, any discriminatory actions by an organization and/or its representatives may damage that organizations ability to grow. Demoralizing questions and comments are never acceptable. For the best interest of the team, it is important to build an environment where all the team members feel welcomed and are celebrated for their achievements, and the unique set of values they bring to the table, regardless of who they are.

NOTES:

1. How does Gender Diversity positively impact your team and organization? Please share an example.

_____
_____
_____

2. How can Socioeconomic Diversity workforce impact your team and organization? Please Share an example.

_____
_____
_____

3. How will Racial Diversity positively impact your organization? Please share an example.

_____
_____
_____

4. How does Educational Diversity positively impact your organization? Please share an example.

_____
_____
_____

5. Is it ever okay to share disparaging jokes with your team members?

_____
_____
_____

6. Is it acceptable to engage in sexually suggestive statements or gestures about the opposing gender? Explain why?

Joe Woodley   Leadership and Team Development Volume 2

JOURNAL

Date:_____

Section 4

Gender Communication

Perhaps one of the most difficult communication skills we must acquire in this era is how men and women communicate with each other, in a way that is respectful and instills a sense of value and honor. You are obligated, both legally and morally, to foster a non- threatening environment.

This requires investing the time to retrain how we see each other and breaking old habits, some of which are subtle or unconscious forms of communication. Perhaps a female counterpart is excluded from a vital conversation and no one notices, or cares to notice. It could be our preconceived ideas about the roles of men and women in society; A male or female joins the team and his ability to perform is instantaneously questioned because of stereotypical attitudes.

How we communicate is just as much verbal as it is nonverbal, and this is where conflict often arises. The percentage of women in the workforce is not going to decline. So, our ability to communicate as professionals and as equals in corporate settings is crucial to the social, economic and community success many of us want to participate in.

A major point of concern should be that almost 50% of women in the workplace feel undervalued by the organizations they work for, their supervisors and the teams they are a part of. These figures are unacceptable, and no organization can build sustained success on such numbers.

Addressing this imbalance requires taking proactive steps through training, honest conversation and deliberate actions to ensure each team member feels included in the process.

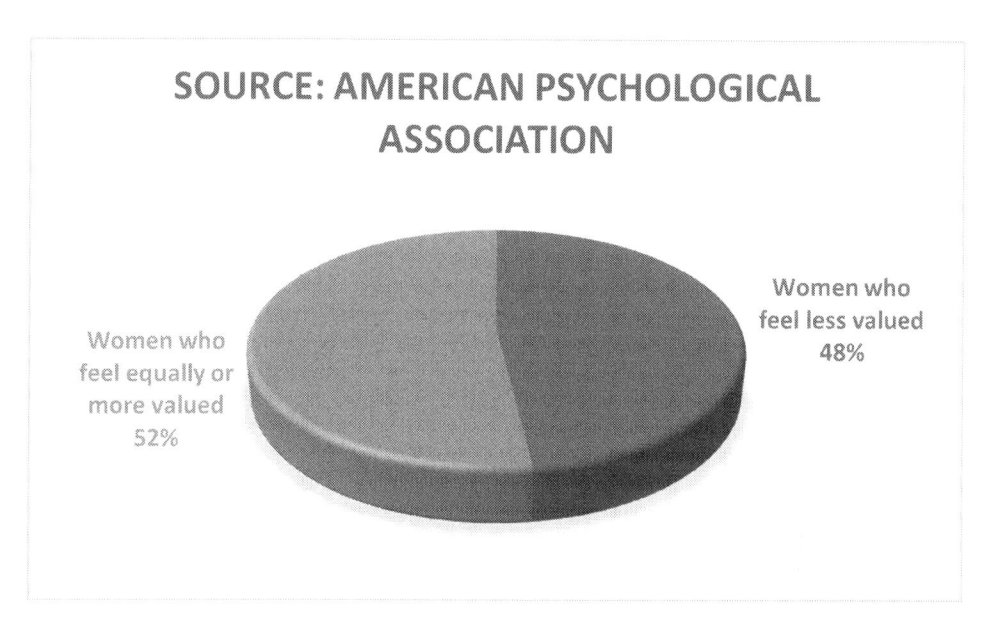

SOURCE: AMERICAN PSYCHOLOGICAL ASSOCIATION

Women who feel equally or more valued 52%

Women who feel less valued 48%

1. Be more intentional about including both genders in the decision- making processes

   _____
   _____
   _____

2. Think before you speak! Ask yourself, if I were a (opposite gender), would I be offended by this conversation

   _____
   _____
   _____

3. Treat every individual on the team with respect

_____
_____
_____

4. Wait until your teammate finishes his statement before responding

_____
_____
_____

5. Avoid making sexually suggestive statements and comments about each other

_____
_____
_____

6. Avoid any interaction that may be deemed as inappropriate or harassment

_____
_____
_____

List 5 ways you and your team can help nurture an environment where every team member feels welcome:

1. _____
_____

2. _____
_____

3. _____
   _____
4. _____
   _____
5. _____
   _____

JOURNAL

Date:_____

Joe Woodley — Leadership and Team Development Volume 2

Session 5

Communication 101

The bedrock of any stable and prosperous organization is grounded in its capability to foster open lines of communication, in every area. Couples that lack effective communication skills, breakup. A government whose officials lack effective communication skills are dysfunctional. And nations that lack effective communication skills go to war with each other. If you want your organization to survive, and progress to a place where it can begin to thrive- it is an imperative that leaders and team members are willing to learn, and implement effective communication skills.

The worst performing organizations are not the ones who are the least talented, or who don't employ the "best and brightest minds" that money can buy. I can assure you that where communication fails, leadership has failed. Great leaders are amazing communicators. Here's the great news. There are many ways to communicate, and communication is a skill that can be taught, and learned. It's not reserved strictly for the most talented. The other bit of great news is that you don't need to say a lot to say a lot. You can learn a great communicator, and your team and organization are counting on you becoming a great communicator.

NOTES:

Specific

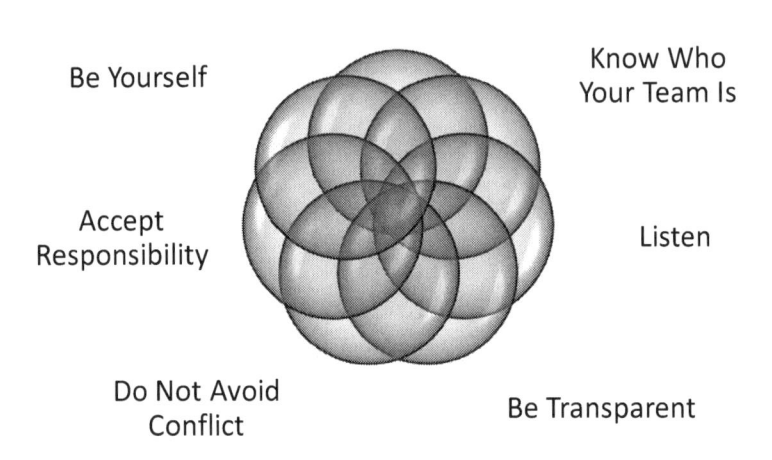

Be Yourself

Know Who
Your Team Is

Accept
Responsibility

Listen

Do Not Avoid
Conflict

Be Transparent

Share examples of how each of these points applies to you, your team, and your organizations ability to succeed.

1. Communicator should invest time in getting to know their teams.

_____
_____
_____

2. They should be willing to listen. Without interrupting.

_____
_____
_____

3. Effective communicators are transparent. They have answers for the questions they are asked.

Joe Woodley   Leadership and Team Development Volume 2

4. They accept responsibility for their failings.

5. Communicators should be specific when providing direction.

6. Communicators who excel do not avoid conflict. They understand that unaddressed conflicts can destroy the effectiveness and productivity of the team.

7. And effective communicators are comfortable being who they are. People can tell when you are being genuine or not.

JOURNAL

Date:_____

Congratulations! You have completed the Volume 2 of Leadership and Team Development Training.

Joe Woodley   Leadership and Team Development Volume 2

Made in the USA
Columbia, SC
07 May 2020